Are You Stuck In Traffic?

A Step-by-Step Guide To A Better Life!

William R. Saunders, Colonel
(USAF Retired)

Are You Stuck In Traffic?

A Step-by-Step Guide To A Better Life!

By

William R. Saunders, Colonel, USAF Retired

Cover Design by Reggie Saunders
Photography by Marci Saunders
Brochure Design by Reggie Saunders
Flyer Design by Reggie Saunders

Printed in the United States of America by www.lulu.com

ISBN 13-Digit: 978-1-4303-0958-1

First Edition

Published 2006

Published by The Saunders Executive Resources Group, LLC, P.O. Box 26095, Macon, GA 31210-9998, U.S.A.
http://TheSaundersExecutiveResourcesGroup.com/index.html

Dedication

This book is dedicated "In Loving Memory" of my mother, Mrs. Sarah Lee Gladden Saunders, my first love and one of the strongest women I know. Thanks for teaching me passion, patience, positive attitude, perseverance and that a "country boy" like me could achieve if I only believe. Mom, the family is doing OK. We miss you so much!

About The Author

Colonel Bill Saunders (USAF Retired) is currently president and managing member of The Saunders Executive Resources Group, LLC, a serviced disabled veteran owned small business. He is a native of John's Island, South Carolina where he graduated from St John's High School in 1972. The colonel is a graduate of Tuskegee University, Tuskegee, Alabama with a bachelor's degree in mechanical engineering (cum laude), a master's degree in business administration from Golden Gate University, San Francisco, California and a Master of Science degree in national resource strategy from the Industrial College of the Armed Forces, Ft Lesly J. McNair, Washington, DC.

Colonel Saunders is a command pilot with more than 3,200 flight hours, a decorated DESERT STORM Veteran with 57 flying missions, a former assistant professor at Howard University, and has held several high-level operational positions at the Pentagon in Washington DC and served as both the Inspector General and Director of Readiness & Homeland Security at the Warner Robins Air Logistics Center, the largest employer in the state of Georgia. At the request of the Honorable Mayor C. Jack Ellis, Colonel Saunders retired from the Air Force in 2004 and served as the Chief Administrative Officer (CAO) for the great City of Macon, Georgia.

Colonel Saunders is a powerful motivational speaker, communicator, and "Out of the Box" thinker. With 32 years of proven leadership and on the motivational speaking circuit since 2005, he has inspired thousands to make a positive difference in their lives with his message of self-empowerment. Through his thought-provoking, participatory, interactive and conversational style, he implores his listeners to dive deep into their psyche in a quest to uncover the root of their problems and to shed light on how they can achieve their goals.

TABLE OF CONTENTS

ACKNOWLEDGEMENTS: 1

INTRODUCTION: 3

ARE YOU STUCK IN TRAFFIC? 7

ARE YOU THE BEST AT WHAT YOU DO? 16

THE GOAL! WHAT IS YOUR GOAL? 25

WHAT IS YOUR PLAN? 34

TELL ME WHO YOU ARE IN 30 SECONDS: 43

WHY ARE YOU SO BUSY? 51

IT'S TIME TO GET UP; NOT LATER…RIGHT NOW! 60

WHAT'S STOPPING YOU FROM ACHIEVING YOUR GOAL? 69

DON'T GIVE UP! 79

CONCLUSION: 89

APPENDIX A: CHAPTER HANDOUTS 91

APPENDIX B: ADDITIONAL INFORMATION 103

Acknowledgements

I would like to just take a moment to formally acknowledge the people who so unselfishly gave of their time and counsel in helping me to be where I am today and to keep me focused on the subject of one day putting pen to paper. "Are You Stuck in Traffic?" is the direct result.

My Mother: For teaching me passion, sensitivity, common sense, good manners and the drive to stay away from the wrong crowd.

My Father: For teaching me clarity of purpose, for teaching me about commitment to community service, about the difference between street smart and book smart and about only being afraid of what I cannot see.

My Wife: For having the patience to put up with me for almost 29 years, especially regarding the journey to find my nitch and my calling in life. It takes a special woman and you are all that!

My Daughter: For providing that positive stroke "Dad, Just Do It." You are a beautiful young lady and I am so very proud of you—we are so much alike—I look forward to partnering with you some day soon. Dad loves you.

My Son: For being the graphic designer behind every pictorial representation of The Saunders Executive Resources Group, LLC. Thank you for showing me to the world with style, clarity and professionalism. I could not have done this without your design expertise and wise counsel.

My Sisters and Brother: For putting up with my non-stop talking as we were growing up but most of all for being competitive, with a willingness to be an achiever and to make Momma proud—we done good! I am proud to be your brother.

Eddie Fyall & Cordell Jenkins: For always being there when I needed you. We have been taking care of each other since elementary school—there is nothing more precious than our friendship.

Bob Dixon, Colonel, USAF Retired: For always checking up on me and providing words of wisdom and encouragement over the many years—you are a true friend.

My brothers/sister's-in-law, cousins, friends/buddy, military family, acquaintances and associates: For personally touching me in your own way as each of you were a gift to accompany me on my life's journey. There is no doubt our path crossed for a reason and I am who I am because of it.

Mr Herbert Dennard & Staff, Host of the Herbert Dennard Show and Publisher of the Georgia Informer, Macon GA: For believing in my vision and for giving me an opportunity to be seen and heard. Thanks for our many conversations.

The Readers: It's because of you that I wrote this book. As I continue to live, I continue to learn from you—don't ever stop teaching me!

Introduction

Life is a journey and just like any journey we all start out at different points. Some of us are born poor. Some of us are born rich. Some of us are lucky enough to have a family that's got enough love to get them through the hard times. Then, there are still others who start out in life not finding the love they need anywhere. No matter where we start out in life, we are all traveling the same road, with only one goal in mind...happiness and fulfillment.

As a conversationalist, I truly enjoy an engaging conversation with my audience. With that in mind, I purposely wrote this book the way that I speak. "Are You Stuck in Traffic?" is a candid conversation with you, the reader—it's just "plain speak." So, for you "grammatically correct" readers, you may find a few syntax issues. My daughter, an elementary school teacher in Maryland, suggested as an option that you read the book "aloud" when confronted with the grammatical arrangement of words in sentences. I wanted to tell you this upfront so that you don't lose sight of the book's purpose. My purpose is to help you with your life's journey by providing proper guideposts that will get you to think; that will provoke thought; that will provoke a positive mental attitude; and ultimately provoke action--all aimed at helping you to reach your goal. It's important to note that there are "no right" or "no wrong" answers in this book with no judgment on my part. I just want you to think effectively and act accordingly.

I started out in life poor on John's Island, SC on a small farm, the oldest of six children and the only boy amongst girls until my little brother arrived on the scene. I like to think of myself as a "country boy." The town I grew up in was in some ways behind the times, and like most residents on John's Island, I didn't have the things that many in America had like running water and electricity in my early childhood years. My overall education was good BUT not good enough to fully prepare me for college engineering. Many times I felt shortchanged and cheated. But fortunately, I was surrounded by some very strong men and women (especially my parents & teachers—I can still call their names) who showed me that it is not where you start out in life that matters, but what you do that will determine your success or failure—it's where you end up.

My grandfather, born in 1892 and one of only a handful of black men at the time, especially from John's Island, SC, with a high school education (think about it--the timeframe is 1910 -1912), read the newspaper everyday from front to back—every article on every page. He read so much that he acquired enough knowledge to become a leader in the community—he was considered intellectually worldly. I thought he was pretty smart. Folks, there is power in reading!

My father, whom I consider to be a self made man, rose independently through the ranks of Charleston, SC politics to become a recognized leader throughout the state. In 1980, he became the sole owner of the only black radio station in the Charleston area (WPAL--Where People Always Listen)—a radio station dedicated to providing blacks and the underserved community access to local, national and world news as well as music and entertainment. Dad knew early about the power of information and worked hard to insure that the listening audience could no longer say "that they didn't know!" Additionally, he was a state commissioner and is a Korean War PURPLE HEART recipient--an honor he received 50 plus years later.

My mother, God bless her heart, a woman to whom I dedicate this book, my first love, showed me passion, patience, respect and what inner strength is all about. She showed me what it really means to be a loving & dedicated parent. She showed me what it means to stay the course, to stay focus and "how just plain common sense can get you where money can't."

Collectively, they showed me that with very little we can accomplish much and that if you believe it, you can achieve it. It is within us all. They all traveled the road of life and didn't allow themselves to get stuck. And if they did get stuck, they didn't stay that way very long.

Many of us are traveling the journey of life, but we're “stuck in traffic.” I hope to inspire those of you who are “stuck in traffic” to get unstuck. I hope to give you the tools that you need to get up and get in control of your life today, right now. If a “country boy” from John's Island, SC can set out on his journey and accomplish his goals, you can too.

Like the majority of folks from my hometown of John's Island SC, we were economically and educationally deprived. The bad and sad part is that many of us didn't know it. I knew it early in my life and to this day, I am still hungry for education.

This book is about making you HUNGRY for knowledge, HUNGRY for awareness and HUNGRY for reaching a position in this country (your goal), no matter what that position is, to make a difference in your life, in people's lives and to minimize or avoid being “stuck in traffic” all together.

Now take hold of my hand and let's walk life's journey together to our final destination: happiness and fulfillment.

Enjoy the book!

CHAPTER 1

Are you stuck in traffic?

Have you ever been stuck in traffic? Did you ever get in your car and think to yourself, "I've got just enough time to make it to where I'm going" and then realize that you're faced with wall to wall traffic and you were, in fact, not going to make it to your destination? How did that make you feel? Were you upset? Were you afraid? Were you angry? Did you start blaming the other folks in their cars, who were stuck in traffic just like you? Did you place the blame on the architects and engineers who designed the highway? Did you think about turning back? Did you think about giving up? Did being stuck in traffic cause you to miss out on a once in a lifetime opportunity? Maybe you were on your way to a job interview or a first date. How long were you stuck in traffic and why didn't you anticipate it? Life's journey is just like one grand highway and unfortunately many of us are stuck in traffic.

What are the things in your life that's got you stuck in traffic? And why didn't you anticipate it?

Is your life where it's been for the past 10 years? Are you stuck in the same old job? Maybe you're working a job you hate or that you love; but it just isn't paying enough to take you where you want to go financially. Are you stuck in the same old relationships? Are you surrounded by people who are not supportive; whose verbal and nonverbal communications not only suggests a non-interest in what you are doing or want to do but is very destructive to your self-image and life progress? Are you stuck? Are you stuck in the same old routine, the same daily grind? Doing the same thing day in and day out, doing the things that are taking you absolutely nowhere? Many of us have to say yes, that we are stuck in traffic and going nowhere fast. The sad thing is that many of us know that we are stuck and we know we need to do something to fix it but for some reason, we don't.

I was en route to Atlanta, Georgia the other day from Macon, Georgia on Interstate 75 northbound because I had a meeting at 6:00 pm. I left at 3:00 pm because I was going to have a late lunch before the meeting and that gave me 3 hours to do it and still arrive on time—with no traffic jams, the drive to Atlanta only takes a little more than an hour from my house. But low and behold, when I got to McDonough, Georgia, traffic was at a complete standstill. The interesting thing here is that I wasn't stressed at all. Because I had anticipated the possibility of traffic and left early, I was feeling relaxed about the situation. But the guy in the car behind me, he was jumping in and out of his car every few minutes. Every time traffic moved 5 feet he jumped out of his car because he was running late for something. He was so frustrated because he failed to anticipate the possibility that there would be traffic. Well, because I had anticipated the possibility of traffic and acted accordingly I was feeling pretty good.

As a matter of fact, I came up with this subject, "Are You Stuck in Traffic?" and recorded it while I was literally stuck in traffic. You see, I was prepared, complete with a recording machine to help occupy my time just for occasions like this. Don't let the traffic jams of your life catch you unprepared. If you are finding yourself stuck in traffic you need to stop right now, think and collect your wits. You need to analyze your situation and then take the proper action on what you can change to prevent being stuck. You need to ask yourself, "What do I need to change in my life to prevent being stuck?" You need to know your priorities. You need to do your homework. You need to study and you need to do it early. Do it right now! Take a vacation, go to school, relax, read, take a train, etc. You've got to be able to analyze your situation and take the proper action. If you take the time to analyze your life right now you may find that you can make some changes that will enable you to avoid being stuck in traffic. You will be able to do the right thing for yourself so that you can be a better person.

Twenty years ago I was stuck in traffic. Twenty years ago I told myself that I wanted to talk, that I wanted to speak for a living, that I wanted a career in public speaking; but I continued to work in professions that did not involve public speaking because of the fear of not being able to put food on the table for me and my family.

Therefore, the majority of my career, albeit a great career, has been centered around "security" and acceptability—being a USAF military officer definitely gave me security and although speaking was involved throughout my career, I never took steps in my journey to become a professional speaker. I didn't even look at the requirements. I was "stuck in traffic."

As I look back, I realize that I could have done many things to pursue my public speaking career while still holding down a job. I could have done part-time public speaking until I made enough money to move into public speaking as a full-time job, but I didn't. If I had explored the other options of pursuing my dream of public speaking for a living, maybe I would have gotten my start 15 years ago, 10 years ago, 5 years ago. Being stuck in traffic can mean many things to many people. For me, being stuck in traffic allowed obstacles to stop me from pursuing my goal; such as not having the money to support my family and not looking at other options that were available to launch my public speaking career. Many of us are faced with similar obstacles that may at the time seem insurmountable. To avoid being stuck in traffic, take the time to explore your situation thoroughly in search of a way to continue to pursue your goal without being stopped by obstacles, whatever those obstacles may be.

Are you surrounded by people who are stuck in traffic?

So many of us are surrounded by a bunch of folks stuck in traffic just like us! Our friends! Our family! Our significant other! Our co-workers! We're just surrounded by a sea of traffic! And what do we get? We get the feeling of normalcy, of complacency. We have to stop and turn this situation around. We have to realize that being "Stuck in Traffic" is not the way we should live our lives. It is not the normal course of life and definitely not the road to success and personal satisfaction. If you find yourself "Stuck in Traffic," what should you do?

1. Stop!

2. Analyze your situation using the worksheets provided in this book and find out how you can get out of traffic. Make it a family and friends affair. Work together to get out of the traffic jam.

3. If all else fails, you need to turn off the noise. What is the noise? The noise is the naysayers stuck in traffic with you. The people who tell you that you don't have the power to change your life. The people who whisper "seeds of doubt" in your ear by their non-action, non-commitment, no encouragement, no pat on the back and no comment. The people who convince you that you are going to fail or question why you even try. You know who they are! You need to get away from folks who are tearing you down. And if you can't get away physically, then make sure you separate yourself mentally. How do you do that? Don't believe a word that the naysayers' speak and don't let their lack of support be a deterrent to achieving your goal. You have the power to change your life. You have the power to get out of traffic.

On the next few pages I will walk you through a series of exercises that will help you get out of traffic and back into the fast lane of life.

STOP! Stop whatever it is that you're doing right now and take stock of your life. Turn off the TV, turn down the radio, and put the kids to bed. Find a quiet space and a moment for yourself and answer the following questions, honestly and candidly.

What does being stuck in traffic mean to you?

What are the situations in your life that have you stuck in traffic? (Is it a dead end job? What about a loveless relationship?)

1.

2.

3.

4.

5.

What are the concrete steps that you can take to make a change to these situations? (Maybe you need to send out resumes every week or begin attending counseling sessions for whatever is bothering you.)

1.

2.

3.

4.

5.

What can you do today, right now, to change your situation?

1.

2.

3.

4.

5.

What is the cost in time, resources and money for you to begin getting out of traffic?

Do you need to spend money on a certificate or degree, so you can find a better paying or more fulfilling job?

Will you have to invest time in going to singles events and parties, to find a loving mate?

What is it that you must invest in order for you to move forward in life?

If you take the time to analyze your life, you may find that you can make some changes that will put your life in balance or minimize being bogged down in the routine.

Again, life is too short and too precious to be stuck in something too long that you know is not good for you. Find ways to make your life better today!

CHAPTER 2

Are you the best at what you do?

Are you operating at your full potential in life? Are you at the top in your field of expertise? Are you the best parent you can be? How about the best friend? No matter what it is that you do or say you want to do, you need to ask yourself if you're the best at what you do. And if you are not the best at what you do, then why not and what are you doing to become the best? As a matter of fact, for those of you who believe emphatically that you are the best at what you do, what are you doing to stay the best? Sooner or later and many times sooner than later, something happens like getting older, health issues, technology changes, or that smart kid from Department XYZ makes you number 2 and worst yet—maybe not even needed.

Are you educating yourself? Are you studying the things you need to study? Do you plan to go back to school? So many folks say they want to accomplish something but they are not striving to be the best at what they do? What is holding you back? If you want to be lawyer, it is impossible to become a lawyer if you never study law, at least not a real lawyer, one licensed by a state board. And if you want to become the best lawyer out there, it is not enough to simply study law; you must live it, eat it, drink it, sleep it and allow it to fill your life. You need to become passionate about law to become the best lawyer! You must become passionate about what you do to become the best at what you do!

Do you know where you are right now? Do you know where you want to go?

Where's your life today? Are you satisfied? Are you happy? Or do you find yourself longing for something more? What is it that you are longing for? In order for us to be the best at what we do we must know where we are today. Are we already the best at what we do? Or, are we languishing in mediocrity? You need to stop and ask yourself if you are doing what it is that you want to do and if not, what is it that you want to do?

Ask yourself, what is it that you do? What is it that you want to become the best at doing?

Twenty-eight years ago I was faced with a situation that forced me to become the best at what I was doing and I mean putting all of me into making me the best. At 22, I was a mechanical engineering degree graduate of Tuskegee University, cum laude (Not bad for a country boy from John's Island, SC). I had a United States Air Force Pilot Training scholarship and up until that point I had never failed at anything. I had always been in the top 5 percent of all my classes. So I arrived at Vance Air Force Base, Enid, Oklahoma in February 1978 and took my first steps into the one year intensive military pilot training program.

Within the first two weeks I was faced with an exam. Now at pilot training, they had a policy that you could not fail three exams without meeting a board. I failed this first exam twice. I was not prepared. Although I knew the material, I did not know the art of military testing, especially differentiating between answers like "as soon as possible and as soon as practical," which clearly suggested to me that I did not know how to study properly for military pilot exams. While others had brothers, cousins, uncles, fathers, neighbors, friends involved with some aspect of flying throughout their childhood and young adult years, I did not—I was once again playing catch-up.

While others would study in groups, I studied alone. It wasn't enough. I had to become the best at what I was doing. I was forced to go back and change my habits and learn new and more effective ways of accomplishing my goals. I had to learn to read the test questions carefully so that I was able to catch the nuances. I had to learn how to study and interpret the meaning of every word related to a particular subject. It was not just about reading the subject matter, but about fully understanding everything, the meaning of every word, to be able to see the page with your eyes closed. I had to become the best at what I was doing. After failing the test twice, I prayed for something better, I prayed for the will and power to get through this. I knew that if I failed the test again or any other test in the pilot program, I would have to meet the board and I would most likely wash out of pilot training school (this would have been a major failure for me, especially with a wife and a 1-year old baby girl). The pressure was on.

So I buckled down, cut out the unnecessary and wasteful things in my life. I allowed myself to be helped by my wife, allowed myself to fully engage in activities with my pilot training classmates (especially as it related to study and preparation for exams), allowed myself to get and stay focused and worked twice as hard with my new skills and habits. I did not fail another test throughout the rest of the 49 weeks in the program. I earned my wings in January 1979.

Have you been in a situation where you were pushed against the wall and forced to bring out your best? I was motivated to push beyond what could have easily discouraged me. What motivates you when you're up against the wall?

What is your motivation?

Why are you doing what you do? What drives you? Is it money? Is it fame and fortune? Are you doing what you do for yourself, or for someone else? Without the right motivation, it is impossible to become the best at what you do. What is the right motivation? The right motivation is love or passion for whatever it is that you do. Without a love and passion for what you do, it is impossible to become the best. How do you know if you love what you do? Good question. Simply ask yourself, 'If I had all the money in the world but had to do one thing for the rest of my life, what would it be?" Folks, ask yourself, if you had all the money in the world, would you still work at that job or would you be doing something else?

So many of us do things because we think we have to, that we don't have a choice. Somebody told us that it was the best thing for us. We believe that if we don't stay at that job or work in a certain field that we won't make any money, that we'll become homeless, that we aren't qualified for anything else or that we won't be able to take care of our family. What is that called? It's called the motivation of fear. We have to analyze our motivation for doing something. If you are doing what you do out of fear, you are not going to be able to be the best at what you do. You have to be motivated by love. You have to come from the heart.

Make a list of what motivates you? Whether your goal is to be the best parent or the best CEO, make a list of your motivations.

1.

2.

3.

4.

5.

What is your attitude?

Attitude is everything! Your attitude can mean the difference between success and failure. Your attitude can mean the difference between getting that job, that promotion, the relationship of your dreams or finding yourself on the losing end of life. What is attitude? Attitude is basically the way you look at and emotionally respond to your world, your life, your problems. It is your outlook. I just love the song by Donnie McClurkin, one of our great gospel singers/vocalists, "We Fall Down, We Get Up." The true measure of a man or woman is how you react when you fall down. Do you want to get up and if you do want to get up, how do you get up? How are you looking at your situation? Do you only see a problem when faced with conflict and adversity or can you see an endless stream of solutions and possibilities? Folks, it's all about attitude. What's your attitude? If you find yourself with an attitude that only leaves you with frustration you need to change your outlook.

Take some time to reflect on your attitude in life. What is your attitude? How do you see your situation? How do you respond to adversity and conflict when trying to accomplish your goals?

What are the road blocks to becoming the best at what you do?

What is stopping you from becoming the best at what you do? What are the roadblocks that seem so immovable? Is it money? Is it lack of willpower? Is it lack of education? Is it lack of contacts? Many of the things that are stopping us are not real and those that are real may not be the immovable boulders we perceive them to be. We need to take the time to analyze our situation and discover what we can do to remove the roadblocks to us becoming the best at what we do.

What are the roadblocks in your way to becoming the best at what you do?

1.

2.

3.

4.

5.

Are you prepared?

Some folks say timing is everything, but when the "doors of opportunity" open for you, are you prepared to go through them? If you say you want to become a famous singer, what have you done to prepare? Did you take voice lessons? Did you practice singing and voice exercises every day? Did you study other accomplished and highly skilled singers? When the opportunity to become a professional singer presents itself, will you be prepared to accept it? When the opportunity to do what you want to do presents itself, are you prepared to take advantage of that opportunity?

If there is something you need to pick up or if there is some type of training you need to pick up, you need to do it now. You need to be prepared!

I'm not the best at what I do, at least not yet. I am not the best motivational speaker out there, but what I'm doing right now is working to be the best at speaking. I am intensely studying the art of speaking and intensely studying the art of communication.

In July 2005, I decided to transition my life so that I could become a motivational speaker. When I made that decision, I made the commitment to focus all of my energy on becoming the best motivational speaker that I could be.

I embarked upon the journey to becoming the best, a journey that requires commitment, discipline, desire and motivation to do what it takes to be the best. You need to do the same. You need to be prepared! Start preparing yourself today.

What are the things you need to do to prepare yourself to become the best?

1.

2.

3.

4.

5.

Who is on your team?

So many folks try to walk the journey of life alone. But we are not meant to walk alone, we are social creatures, we can't do it by ourselves no matter how much we think we can. So we have to reach out to those around us so that they can help us be our best. Who is on your team? You have to take the time to analyze your situation and find out who is on your side and who is not. Who is on your side and what can they do to help you become the best? Make yourself accountable to someone. Tell a supportive loved one what you want to achieve and allow them to hold you accountable for doing the things you need to do to achieve your goals and become the best at what you do. Make a list. Make a list of the people you know you can count on to be in your corner as you walk this new path to excellence.

Who is on your team?

1.

2.

3.

4.

5.

Take the time to make yourself the best at whatever you want to be. Again, life is too short. Take advantage of what's available to help you achieve your best.

If your best is a "D" or if your best is an "F", I love you, and you should love yourself; but if your best is an "A" and you got a "D" or "F" then you ought to be dissatisfied. Getting a "D" when you can do better is unacceptable!

It's time to stop all the excuses, all the reasons why you can't do something; especially for those things that are within your control like study, attitude and doing your homework.

Stop for a moment and analyze your situation. Find ways to make yourself the best today!

CHAPTER 3

The Goal! What is your Goal?

What is your goal? As a matter of fact, is it your goal? Or is it someone else's goal? Is your goal clearly defined? Is your goal achievable? Is your goal measurable? Is your goal realistic? Is your goal sustainable?

The first step in achieving anything on our journey is to know our goal. Is your goal to be a better parent? The best in your field? To get a job? To get a degree? You need to define specifically what it is that you want out of life. You cannot be vague with this first critical step in making your life better. To say you want to get "a job" is not very clear. You need to ask yourself, what kind of job? After you have decided and brought clarity to what exactly your goal is in life you then need to ask yourself, is your goal realistic? Is your goal achievable? If you say you want to be an astronaut and you know it takes 20 years to achieve that goal and you are 60 years old, which may not be a realistic goal. You need to assess your skills, abilities and sensibilities and juxtapose them against your goal and ask yourself if your goal is achievable.

Now, the next question is something most of us never consider. Is your goal really your goal? Now I know most of you are telling yourselves, of course it is my goal. But you would be surprised to discover that there are a lot of folks in this world trying to achieve goals that are not really their goals. Let me explain. When we were children, we had the belief that anything was possible. As children we were not yet infected with a limited and scarcity mentality. We could not conceive of the possibility that we could not achieve something. We were free.

In this freedom of thought and confidence, we may have told a parent or an older sibling that we wanted to be a President, a Pilot, a Lawyer, a Judge, a Police Officer or whatever it was we believed we could achieve and because of their own fear, they may have discouraged us. They may have told us to lower our expectations. They may have tried to 'protect us' from disappointment and failure. They may have suggested something safer or more in line with what they believed was possible for us to achieve. The result? Many of us are pursuing goals for the wrong reason. Many of us are pursuing goals that are the goals of someone else. We need to seriously analyze our "current goal" and make sure that "this goal" is truly "our own."

If you believe it, you can achieve it!

It is absolutely crucial that you believe that you can achieve your goal. No matter what it is, you must believe that you are capable of achieving your goal. Without belief, without faith, your goal will be out of reach. Have you ever noticed that people who believe that they are unlucky always seem to have no luck? Think about it. Do you have a friend, a relative, a coworker who holds some deeply felt negative belief? If you look at their lives, you will notice that no matter what they do they always seem to validate their belief. If they belief they can't get a raise, for some reason, no matter how hard they work they never get a raise. Even if everyone else in the company got a raise they will be the only one who doesn't get a raise.

What I'm saying folks is that if you believe something hard enough, you will manifest it in your life, positive or negative. And guess what, if you believe you are nice looking, by whatever standards, others will believe in you also or at least try to figure out what makes you believe you are so nice looking. If you believe that you can do the job, then you will, especially if given the proper training and proper tools to execute on this belief.

Is your goal measurable?

Have you ever started the New Year with a list of resolutions? Of course you have. We all have. When the New Year kicks in we set all types of goals. We want to lose weight. Get in shape. Get a new job. Make more money. But the one thing we fail to consider is, are our new goals measurable. And if our new goals are measurable, how do we measure them? Let's look at this for a second.

In order for something to be measurable, you must have a starting point? So, as I always say, in my John's Island, South Carolina accent... "You gotta know where you at." You need to ask yourself, where are you starting from right now? Where are you starting from today? Then you need to ask yourself, where do you want to go?

If you are still with me, folks, you need to know two things before you start your journey towards your goal. You need to know where you are and where you want to go. Then, you need to take the two and connect the dots. You need to connect the starting point of where you are and the end point of your goal. If your goal, for instance, is to get to the other side of the river, you need to know where you are on this side of the river. If you don't know where you are on this side, then you don't know that if you just move one half mile further east, you could just walk across to the other side of the river or you might just come across a bridge. The reality of this statement as it relates to where I am from in South Carolina is that at low tide in many of our rivers, you can always find a spot that will allow you to cross without getting your clothes or your feet wet. You must pay attention to where you are or said my way, "where you at!"

You could be lost in downtown Atlanta while trying to get to the CNN Center. The key here is that your goal is to get to the CNN Center; but you don't know where you are. And if you don't know where you are, you'll drive around all day. Maybe you'll only waste an hour or two hours and then all of a sudden the light will come on. The light will come on and say "stop for a second, let's just pull the car to the side of the road and ask somebody or you know what, pull out a map." This new found light in your mind will tell you to pull out a map and find out where you are. If you know where you are and you know the CNN Center is 5 blocks away, all you have to do is "connect the dots." Folks, we have got to "connect the dots." We must figure out where we are in relation to our goal. If you want to be a lawyer and you never went to college, your goal is at least seven years away. If you want to be an engineer and you don't have a degree in engineering it is going to take you at least 4 years to get there, provided you have all the prerequisites completed when you start. What is your goal? And how far are you from achieving it? What are the things that you need to do to achieve your goals?

What are the roadblocks to achieving your goals?

What are the roadblocks to achieving your goal? What's in your way? Is it you? Is it somebody else? What is it?

Do you lack motivation? Are you lacking the will to move forward on the things that will make you successful? If you lack motivation, you need to ask yourself, why? If this is in fact your goal, why aren't you motivated to pursue it? What can you do to motivate yourself to move forward?

1. Clarify your goal and be specific.
2. Don't get overwhelmed. Take baby steps. I am reminded here that "the only way to successfully eat an elephant is one bite at a time," or that "the journey of a thousand miles begins with a single step."
3. Do one small thing today to move yourself closer to your goal.

Are you exhausted? Do you find it hard to take the steps necessary in order to accomplish your goals because you are too tired at the end of the day to do anything else? If you're finding yourself exhausted and burnt out, take time out and rest. You must first take care of your physical and mental health before you can effectively accomplish anything beyond the daily and minimum requirements of everyday life. Once again take baby steps. "Rome wasn't built in a day." And it is impossible to accomplish any worthy goal overnight. Take baby steps and know that you are one step closer to your goal. If you want to become a great pianist you don't accomplish that overnight. Becoming a great pianist is accomplished one note at a time.

What about procrastination? So many of us are guilty of putting off until tomorrow what we know we need to do today. What about you? How often do you find yourself avoiding the tasks you know you need to do? Procrastination is a dream killer--it puts you in the category of a person who just talks and talks and talks and at the end of the day has done absolutely nothing, at the end of the year has done nothing, at the end of ten years has done nothing and at the end of his life's journey has done nothing. The bottom line is that at the end of the journey, you wish you had "done this" or "done that." There is nothing worse, in my opinion, than to wish you had done something, especially when you had the time to do it. Don't kill your dream with procrastination. You have the power to take action. Don't delay—do it today—right now.

Are you qualified? Surprisingly, many of us fail to even consider the fact that we may not be qualified for what we set out to do. We've all seen American Idol. So many young people competing for the same prize...to become the next American Idol. But surprisingly many of them are not qualified singers—they did not have the physical attributes (in this case, the singing voice) required to be a professional singer. Now for those who had the singing voice, why did they fail? Because they did not properly prepare—some chose the wrong songs, some chose the wrong outfits to annunciate their whole person, some didn't study or fully understand the judging criteria, some didn't believe they could win, and some came for the wrong reasons (you can probably think of many more).

We have to prepare ourselves to accomplish our goal. If you want to become a doctor, you cannot accomplish that goal if you are not qualified. What do you need to do to become qualified? You need to study human biology. You need to go to college. You need to go to medical school--and to get accepted to medical school, you need to have a great grade point average (GPA) from your college days, especially in the medical subjects. You need to stop right now and ask yourself, am I qualified for what it is that I want to accomplish? If not, what is it that I need to do to become qualified?

The following questions should help you accomplish your goal:

What is your goal? Be clear and specific with you answer.

What is your starting point? Where are you in relationship to your goal today?

What are the roadblocks to achieving your goal?

1.

2.

3.

4.

5.

6.

7.

8.

9.

10.

How can you overcome your roadblocks?

1.

2.

3.

4.

5.

6.

7.

8.

9.

10.

CHAPTER 4

What is your plan?

What is your plan? How do you plan to accomplish the goals you say you want to achieve? It is absolutely critical that you have a plan? If you don't have a plan, then you need to stop right now and get one. You need to start putting together a plan today.

What is a plan? A plan is a scheme or method of acting and/or proceeding to obtain some objective or goal. What is your scheme or method of acting? If you say your goal is to become physically fit or to eat healthier, then what is your scheme or method of acting? What is your plan? Do you actually exercise? Do you actually eat fruits and vegetables? Or do you sit on the couch watching TV and eating Ding Dongs, ice cream and cupcakes (not that these foods don't taste good or have value)? Folks, we just need to get serious. We need to figure out if we have a plan and if we have a plan, are we working it?

Is your plan written down somewhere? Or are you working your plan from memory? As you all know, the mind can be a tricky place. You may say to yourself that your plan for tomorrow is to set aside time to study but then the next day you completely forget because some more entertaining task distracted you. Don't depend on your memory for keeping track of your plan. You need to write it down in detail. Be specific. And you need to track what it is that you do everyday to accomplish your plan. The specifics of your plan, much like your goal, must be realistic, doable or achievable. It should not be daunting or overwhelming because if it is, you are not going to like it and you are not going to do it because of the frustration involved. You want a plan that eventually becomes a part of you. You need to refer to your plan everyday, making sure that it still fits with your objective, your goal.

What are the steps in your plan? What are the actions that you need to take to accomplish your plan? In the previous chapter, we mentioned that if you want to be a pianist, that goal is accomplished one note at a time. The journey of a thousand miles is accomplished with the first step. If you want to be a pianist, you first must have access to a piano to practice on or at least have access to a keyboard. Then you need to get lessons. Maybe even some books. And most importantly, you need practice, practice, practice and study, study, study. Folks, you have to do your homework. This is the same with any goal, no matter what it is. You must understand this process to achieve your goal.

In order for you to create an effective plan, you first need to find out everything you need to know about your goal. How do you do that? Study other people who have already accomplished what you want to do. As I have come to realize in life and many of you reading this book may also realize, there is really not a whole lot of new or original ideas out there today—somebody has or is successfully doing what you want to do or doing something pretty close to what you want to do. Who are these people and how did they get to be where they are?

Pay attention to their whole story, especially the periods of times in their lives where they may have failed. Pay attention to what they did to pick themselves up from this failure. Pay attention to what motivated them to try again. Pay attention to everything related to their goal and their plans to achieve their goal. What are all the things related to what you do that must or should be considered? Read books about your goal. Read books and articles about the people who have already accomplished the thing that you want. Read books about those who failed and why they didn't get back in the game. Read books about your industry and related industry.

Attend conferences, workshops and seminars that inform and allow you to network with people doing what you want to do. Folks, please don't underestimate the power of networking. There is an old saying, "you never really know who you are talking to or who is listening," so when you talk to people, make sure you are on par, and make sure you say the right things.

I have personally received a lot of help, guidance, and mentoring from folks that I just met because of just being sincere and honest about who I am and what I want to do. My gut feeling is that people genuinely want to help others—look for these types of people in your profession or whatever endeavor you find yourself engaged.

You must know everything about your goal. If you want to be a lawyer, you need to ask yourself, what is it a lawyer does? What type of lawyer do I want to be? A lawyer who specializes or one who generalizes? You must ask yourself, "What is your passion?" Will I like being a lawyer? How much does a lawyer get paid? How many lawyers are in your local area? How many of them are doing well? How many of them specialize? What is the perception of lawyers in your area? Does this matter? How does a lawyer get a job? What types of liabilities are there to being a lawyer? And folks, you should never stop asking yourself these questions. Don't step out there not knowing the basics. This will only hinder you.

What are you doing with your plan?

Are you working your plan? When was the last time you pulled out and reviewed your plan? Is your plan an old plan? Does your plan need to be updated to fit the current situation? Do you know where your plan is? Is your plan readily available? Is it accessible? In today's terms, is your plan on your computer, laptop, or flash/jump drive? The key here is that you have access to your plan no matter where you are. Does your plan include a 'to do' list? Are you checking off tasks on your 'to do' list? Do you have a 'to do' list? How difficult is your plan? Is it realistic? I gotta ask this question again, is the plan yours? Or is it someone else's plan? Have you been achieving your goal or accomplishing your 'to do' list without having to refer to your plan?

Many of us have goals and plans but lack the action necessary to make it happen. We can have all the plans in the world but if we don't take any action, we will never accomplish anything.

In order to make sure that you will take action on your plan, you need to make sure your plan is manageable and normal for you? For example, if you say you want to begin an exercise program, is it realistic for you to get up at 5:30 AM everyday? If you normally get up at 5:30 AM and have some experience working out this time of morning, in the cold, in the dead of winter, by yourself, then yes, this may be a realistic goal. But if you usually sleep in until 10:00 AM on weekdays and 1:00 PM on weekends and you can't walk 10 feet, then this may not be a realistic goal for you. We need to be honest with ourselves. Is your plan realistic and manageable for you?

I was always told that no matter what, "you must run your own race;" don't run someone else's race. If you can't run fast, run slow or jog; if you can't run at all, then walk and be the fastest walker in your neighborhood; if you can't be the fastest walker, just walk. The key here is to work out at your own pace to avoid burn out. Remember, you need to take baby steps so that you won't become overwhelmed, give up or procrastinate.

Many of us don't take action on our plan because we have bitten off more than we can chew. We have too much on our plate. How much is on your plate? If you are feeling overwhelmed by the thought of your plan, it may be that you have too much on your plate. Prioritize your plan. What are the most important items in your plan? Do the most important things first. Don't put the cart before the horse. And most importantly don't be afraid to modify your plan as needed. If you are finding that you are not able to accomplish the things you want in the allotted amount of time or in the order you originally planned, then don't be afraid to change your plan and begin again.

Below are some questions designed to help you create and implement your plan.

What is your goal? Write down your goal from the previous chapter.

Now, what is your plan to achieve your goal?

What are the major steps you need to take to accomplish your plan? Don't worry about the priority, just brainstorm, just put down your thoughts.

1.

2.

3.

4.

5.

From these major steps in your plan, what is the order of priority for each step, complete with all the minor details that must be accomplished? Break down the major steps into a series of tiny steps. For example, if you need to go back to school, maybe the first step is to figure out which school you want to go to, followed by cost to attend.

1.

2.

3.

4.

5.

What can you do everyday to work your plan? Write down the things you can do everyday to work you plan. For example, if you want to become a pianist, you can practice for 15 minutes everyday (time management).

1.

2.

3.

4.

5.

CHAPTER 5

Tell me who you are in 30 seconds

Can you tell me who you are in 30 seconds. I need you to be very succinct and I need you to be very articulate. I need no stuttering. I need no stammering. I need you to tell me who you are in 30 seconds. What value do you offer a particular client and can you market/sell yourself in 30 seconds? If you're looking for employment, what value do you bring to the table? What value do you bring to the company? If you're selling a product or you're selling a service, why should I purchase your product? Why should I purchase your service? Again, can you tell me who you are in 30 seconds?

Let's say I'm doing some hiring and I have three slots and 100 applicants applied. I have the top ten applications on my desk right now, and by the way, you made the top ten. You made the top ten, but guess what folks, your resume and your bio looks the same as everybody else's. So what differentiates you from everyone else?

It comes down to the art of communication. I want you to be able to tell me who you are in 30 seconds because that's all you got. All you have is 30 seconds to tell me who you are, because I'm going to make my decision on whether I hire you or whether I purchase your service or whether I purchase your products based on how you talk to me, on how well you articulate yourself and are you confident about yourself and what you are telling me? Additionally, for those of you who haven't figured it out, this 30 seconds ALSO involve your non-verbal communications skill (body language, demeanor, eye contact, dress, confidence, etc)—you must look the part! Thirty seconds is a long time if you are prepared! If you are not prepared, 30 seconds is NOT a long time!

Do you know who you are?

We need self awareness. We need to know exactly who we are and what we offer the world. Do you know where you fit? Do you know what your nitch is? This is not just on a physical level but also on the level of integrity, common sense, good manners, sincerity, loyalty, character and honesty, just to name a few. Whenever you are selling a service, product or applying for a job you are not just selling that service, product or your skills; but you are also selling YOU. You must be able to sell yourself. You need to understand what you offer as a person. Are you always on time? Never miss a deadline? Are you a team player? Are you easy to get along with? Many of us forget that we are part of the package and we need to be able to tell people in 30 seconds what it is that we offer. I am reminded here of an old ancient proverb, written around 500 BC, by Sun Tzu in the book "Art of War," which states that you must "know thy enemy, know thy self." And many times, the enemy lies within—the enemy is you! Don't sell this fact short because this is where many of us fail. Don't just study the enemy, study yourself, study your friends, study your family and do it on a continuous basis. Remember that each day can bring you something that you didn't know the day before. You got to know yourself!

What do you offer that others don't?

What is the value of what you offer? How will it benefit the person you are selling it to? If you're selling vacuum cleaners, does that vacuum cleaner clean better than others? If you are applying for a job, are you more knowledgeable in your field than others? You need to be specific and you need to be accurate. But you also need to do it quickly and clearly. There's not a lot of time to make a solid first impression. And if you want that first impression to land you the job, to garner you the sale, you must have absolute confidence in the value you bring to others.

The most difficult question or should I say challenge for me as it relates to being a professional motivational speaker is "determining what is my value?" And this determination is based on what I bring to the table, based on my credentials, based on my qualifications, based on industry standards and most of all, based on my passion, my motivation for being in the speaking business. You must know your value. You must know that you can make a difference for your clients, even if it's small as long as it is a positive difference.

For example, if a company has 100 customer service employees and they would like to contract my services regarding a seminar on "The Art of Exceptional Customer Service," I offer them this: I can't change all of your employees, but what if I can get 10% of your employees to be more proactive, to work harder, to go back to school, to anticipate your needs, to be team players, to accept leadership roles, and enhance the profitability of your company, what value would you place on such a return on your investment in my services? Always be prepared to answer this question!

Don't be caught off guard

If you are not able to tell me who you are in 30 seconds then I know the following:

- You are not prepared
- You didn't do your homework
- You didn't study
- You didn't analyze your audience: potential client, customers, employer, etc
- You didn't analyze the situation
- And you definitely didn't anticipate the question

You need to be prepared. You must find out what is it that your potential client, customer or employer needs and wants? You must anticipate obstacles and challenges. In order to do this you have to study. You have to do your homework. Don't be caught off guard!

Create and practice your 30 second commercial

It's time for you to get prepared.

Write down all the qualities and skills that you bring to the table as an individual or business.

1.

2.

3.

4.

5.

Additionally, make a list of your accomplishments and awards.

1.

2.

3.

4.

5.

Now using the information you listed, create a thirty second commercial.

Example: I am Colonel Bill Saunders, USAF Retired, 32 years of dedicated service to this country, 13 months of running the 5th largest city in Georgia—Macon, Georgia. I'm a Command Pilot, 3,200 plus flying hours, a DESERT STORM veteran, 57 missions, Pentagon tested, Assistant Professor, Howard University, Inspector General and Director of Readiness/Homeland Security, Warner Robins Air Logistics Center, Tuskegee University graduate, mechanical engineer, cum laude. And oh yeah, President/CEO/Founder/Managing Member of "The Saunders Executive Resources Group, LLC," a serviced disabled veteran-owned small business, founded July 19, 2005. My passion is to make a positive difference in people's lives through motivation and personal empowerment. Can you feel me?

Now you try....Go ahead, let's write it out; that's right, right now! I left you lots of space.

Write "who you are in 30 seconds." Remember, this is your 30 seconds commercial:

Now that you've created your 30 second commercial you need to practice, practice, and practice. You need to get in front of the mirror. You need to memorize your commercial. You need to talk to yourself. You need to tell yourself who you are in 30 seconds and if you have children, you need to talk to your children. Talk to your significant other. Talk to your friends and have them evaluate you. Don't be afraid of receiving feedback. If anything, you should fight for feedback, especially if constructive. Then test it out on prospective clients/employers at your next networking event.

CHAPTER 6

Why are you so busy?

So you're too busy? Tell me, why is that? Why is it that you're so busy? Tell me, what is going on in your life that you are at a point where you are just so busy? You're so busy that you don't have time for anything. You don't have time to go back to school. You don't have time to take your kids to Burger King or McDonald's or even to the park. You don't have time to get yourself some training. You don't have time to get yourself into a physical fitness program. Why are so many of us too busy to do the most important things in our lives? Are you watching too much TV? Spending too much time daydreaming or gossiping on the phone? How do you spend your time? How do you utilize the time in your day? Do you have your priorities straight? Do you find that you were so busy all day that you didn't have time to get anything done? You've heard that before. "I was so busy today that I didn't get anything done." How is that possible? That's because we don't have our priorities straight. We are not doing first what needs to be done. We're spending too much time doing what we "want" to do instead of what we "need" to do. Or, maybe, we are afraid or just avoiding the hard work of doing the things that need to be done.

What are your priorities?

What are your priorities? What are the things that you need to do to make your life better? If you want to go back to school, what are the actions, the priorities that need to be taken care of in order for you to go to school? Do you want to get a better paying job? What are the priorities? If you want that great job with great pay and benefits, you don't spend your evenings watching reality TV instead of revising your resume, taking classes, networking with companies, attending seminars, attending job fairs or searching the want ads. You don't sit around doing nothing productive if you have your priorities straight. You have to know what your priorities are. If you made a list of actions to accomplish in your plan, then now is the time to prioritize those actions. What are the most important steps? In other words, what is it that you need to do first? What is it that can be put off until another time? You can't do everything all at once. And if you try to do everything at once you're going to get overwhelmed and feel tempted to give up. I don't want you to give up folks. So please get your priorities straight.

What are your time wasters?

What is it that you're doing that you really don't need to do? Are you spending too much time watching TV? Too much time washing the dishes or cleaning the house? Okay, that was a surprise, right? I was just checking to see if you are paying attention. Yes, we need to wash the dishes and clean the house but even that can be a time waster—it's all about time management folks. Some folks will use very valid necessary responsibilities as an excuse for why they cannot move forward in their lives.

Do you really need to vacuum your home three times a day? Do you really need to wash the dishes twice a day? Do you need to wash clothes everyday? Maybe some days you can use disposable plates and save time. Is the fact that you need to do laundry a valid roadblock to your returning to school? You need to ask yourself, how are you wasting your time?

Some of us spend lots of time helping others. It is absolutely wonderful to help others but not at the expense of yourself. You may be spending too much time volunteering your services. Spend some of that time on you--you are also a worthy cause. You just may have too much "on your plate." In the past year, I have personally reduced my participation in many organizations, albeit great organizations, because they took up too much of my time. This was very hard to do BUT very necessary if you want to stay focus and achieve your goal. Don't let other people's time override yours—I want you to think about this statement for a minute. Similarly, if you find that you are spending time on things that must be done and cannot be delayed, then you need to consider delegating some of that responsibility.

Learn to reach out for help. And you know what, the sad part about this is that this scenario is so true, especially for working mothers. I don't mean to just focus on mothers but if you don't delegate some of these responsibilities, your kids or significant other will continue to allow you to do all the work.

Sometimes it's not their fault, especially if you think you are the only one who can do the work correctly and at a certain time—ya'll know what I am talking about. Maybe your children or significant other can wash the dishes and clean the house—give them chores and responsibilities—if your kids are not babies, have them make their own beds, have them clean their own rooms, wash their own clothes, and pick up after themselves. Teach your teenager how to prepare a meal that is not too tasking so that you won't have to do it after work. Better yet, ladies, teach your spouse to cook and maybe even how to grocery shop. Let your family help you!

Or, maybe you can hire someone to do those chores for you, if you have the money. If your commute to work is 2 hours, maybe you can take the train or bus instead and use that time to study or do whatever you need to do to accomplish your goals and plan. Folks, this is sound advice and if you are not doing this type of time management with your life, you are selling yourself short. It's time to make "time management" a priority.

You need to find the time

It is absolutely critical that you find the time to do the things that will make your life better. Stop for a moment and analyze your situation. If you take the time to analyze your life, you may find that you can make the time to take care of you, your family, etc. Life is too short and again too special to be so busy everyday of the week. Take something "off your plate" today. Learn how to "SAY NO" when and where you can! If you want to get busy, get busy with life, otherwise you're going to wakeup one day and find your life filled with unhappiness—find yourself an old man or old woman wishing you had taken the time to fix your life.

If you are reading this book, you are still living and that says to me that you still have time to maybe fix something or do something that you have always wanted to do. And you know what? You might live tomorrow and the next day and the next. I have said it before, "If you got something to do, do it today, right now!"

As I analyze my life, there are a lot of things that I would do different. I was the guy who always fixed it. I was always busy. I never was "not busy". My busy life even kept me from coming home on time and spending precious quality time with my family. At work, if there was a task that needed to be done, I did it. If someone needed to go home, I let them go.

I taught at Howard University from 86' until 89' and I had workers there that I let go home early every Friday or whenever it looked like it was convenient like on a slow day. And low and behold every Friday, as soon as they left, unscheduled events started immediately and I found myself all of a sudden so busy doing their work, answering the phones (oh those phone calls) and taking care of walk-in customers. Administrative work can be very time consuming and tasking, especially when you have your own responsibilities to complete—my "hats off" to all administrative employees. I eventually ended up with elevated...well, high blood pressure, which was a wakeup call that made me say "guess what, I'm going home today, you guys stay." I took time to relax, go to the gym, hit the track, visit the sauna and you know what, it felt good and my blood pressure went back to a normal range. Folks, it's about prioritizing your activities.

At that time I was very prioritized in work stuff, but not my personal life. If life has got you so busy that you don't have time for your kids, your significant other, or your friends simply because you're trying to get to that next level in your job, career or because you're chasing fortune and fame, you have to realize that your life needs reprioritizing—that your life needs to be about living.

Although making money is a major issue for many individuals, for many families, that is not what life is about. Life is about the things that cannot be bought or sold...love, family and happiness.

Take an inventory of your life right now. Pull out pen and paper and write down everything you do each day. BRAINSTORM this list, don't try to analyze this list right now, just get it down on paper. Don't short change yourself either. Include everything you do.

1.

2.

3.

4.

5.

6.

7.

8.

9.

10.

From the list of things you do everyday, write down how you can eliminate, delegate or minimize time spent on these things.

1.

2.

3.

4.

5.

6.

7.

8.

9.

10.

Now, what I want you to do is write down a list of things that are time wasters in your life.

1.

2.

3.

4.

5.

6.

7.

8.

9.

10.

Now from this list, write down how you will eliminate, minimize or delegate these time wasters.

1.

2.

3.

4.

5.

6.

7.

8.

9.

10.

CHAPTER 7

It's time to get up; not later...RIGHT NOW!

It is time to get up right now! Why are so many of us still sitting down not achieving our goals in life? Why are you not motivated? Are you tired? Why are you still sitting down when you have things to do folks? We need to be getting up and doing the right things to make our lives better. It's time to get up. No more procrastination. No more sitting on yesterday's laurels, it's time to make that goal a reality.

it's time to have a starting point and to connect that starting point to your goal. Make it happen. No more talking folks. You've heard the saying, "you can talk the talk; but it's time now to walk the walk." It's time to get up. It's time to have some clarity of purpose for your life. It's time to make yourself the best at what you do.

It's time to rise above mediocrity. Stop being "just okay." Stop being "just average." Strive to excel in life. Strive to be the best at what you do. It's time to make yourself stand out. Stand out in the workplace. Stand out in class. Be the best at whatever you're doing. It's time to go back to school. If you don't have time, make time. It's time to learn that trade and earn yourself the best grade in whatever class you are taking.

God accepts U-turns

If you find yourself going in the wrong direction, stop and turn around. I was driving down Interstate 75 southbound coming from Macon, Georgia to Warner Robins, Georgia, and there was a big sign in big black and white lettering on the side of the road that said, "If you find yourself going in the wrong direction, God accepts U-turns." Folks, everything I see or hear everyday is an opportunity to enhance myself professionally and socially, just like this sign.

I'm saying to you, that if you find yourself going in the wrong direction, you need to stop. You need to stop right now and turn yourself around. If you know that you're doing the wrong thing and it's going to get you nothing, it's going to bring you "no value," then it's time to stop. If you know you need some education, if you know you need a certificate to do your job, then ladies and gentlemen, it's time to stop and go get that certificate. The goal you want will not be achieved if you continue on the track that's taking you nowhere. It's time to put your life in order. So many of us are going in the wrong direction and refuse to make a U-turn. You don't have to continue on the wrong path. We all have a chance to turn around.

Additionally, many of us allow ourselves to get caught up in the past--past mistakes, past failures and past hurts. Although you can learn from the past, you need to stop operating in the past because that is going to "stop you" and get you nowhere. You need to operate from today, right now. Today is what you have the power to control—you can't fix yesterday, no matter how hard you try, you can't change it.

When I first started out in the speaking business, I mistakenly believed that people would hire me as a speaker simply on the merits of my past accomplishments as a Colonel in the military and as the Chief Administration Officer (CAO) for the great city of Macon, Georgia. So when after four months of being in business, the phone wasn't ringing and I wasn't getting the jobs that I thought I should, I got frustrated. I couldn't figure out why folks weren't responding the way I had envisioned. Whatever the reasons, I needed to do some more homework. By getting busy studying the folks who were doing the things that I wanted to do, I learned what I needed to do to be successful in my public speaking career. My involvement and subsequent membership with the National Speakers Association (NSA) and the local NSA, Georgia Chapter, definitely contributed to my understanding of what it takes to become a successful public speaker. NSA is the leading educational and networking organization for professional speakers.

I realized that people wanted to see my work as a speaker. I had made a mistake. I spent four months pursuing a speaking career with my priorities in the wrong order. I didn't have a portfolio or a proper track record as a speaker. So what did I do? Well, I didn't stop and give up just because I had made a mistake and spent four months going in the wrong direction. I didn't despair over the past. When I realized that I was going in the wrong direction, I stopped, checked my life map, got good directions, and then turned around so that I could begin heading in the right direction.

I began to go out and speak for free to create a portfolio and a "public speaking" track record. Every opportunity I had to do a speaking engagement, I did. After being interviewed for a local TV show, I was given a chance to come back and do a weekly 4-5 minute motivational TV series on the subject of my choosing—this was suppose to last for 2-3 weeks. Well, it lasted almost five months and gave me additional visibility in the community.

Folks, you never know what's going to happen for you unless you put yourself out there to be seen and heard. I got a chance to meet some local videographers and as a result, I was able to produce some CDs and DVDs. And by the way, I began writing this book! I got out there and connected to the folks that I saw accomplishing the things that I wanted to do. And I'm suggesting to you, that you do the same. Don't let "past errors" stop you. Seize today and move in the right direction. Focus on the things that are within your control.

Focus on the 1%

You want to achieve a goal and somebody is telling you that it's not possible. A lot of folks (maybe as high as 99%) say that what you want is not a possibility. As a matter of fact, most folks are telling you that you have a slim chance of success. Folks, I have believed for a long time that if there is a 1% chance of making something happen, put all of your energy into that 1%. Don't spend all of your energy on that 99% chance that it won't happen. Put all of your energy into doing the things that can make that 1% chance a reality.

As I mentioned earlier, I'm a "country boy." I was born and raised on John's Island, SC and graduated from St John's High School. The island was not a rich place by any stretch of the imagination but I sure enjoyed those days. As I reflect back, we (the black community) were economically deprived and definitely educationally deprived (at least on a national exposure level) with many of us working on the farms, in the fields to make ends meet. BUT you know what, I didn't realize we were economically or educationally deprived because I was surrounded by a community of folks that lived and looked just like me and were not exposed to anything different.

I didn't come to the realization that we were economically and educationally deprived until I started reading and wow, do I love to read. My grandfather loved to read and he read the newspaper from front to back everyday—he was mentally and intellectually worldly—this worldliness earned him the respect as a community leader. This same love for reading exposed me to the world, to world events and put a hunger in me to improve my position in life, to work hard to reach a position in America where I could make a difference in people's lives. Additionally, this love put a hunger in me to achieve financial security, to take care of my family and to avoid the pitfalls of drugs, crime and that defeatist mentality that captured the attention of so many economically deprived youth, especially black males.

This awareness, this exposure through reading, showed me exactly where I "did not" want to be (no jail, no drugs, and definitely not working hard everyday from pay check to pay check), so I promised myself that I would always strive to be near the top with anything I was involved with—I made sure I stood out in the crowd. I was the oldest of six kids and I promised my mother that that I would make her proud—I feel in my heart of hearts that I accomplished this task. Growing up economically deprived on John's Island could have made it very easy to go down the wrong road of life—ya'll know what I am talking about!

Although many families were strong and successful in their own right, despite the obstacles they faced, I saw most folks, working hard all their lives for little more than the minimum amount of money that was needed to survive.

In my own case, after graduating from high school, I began working for a local factory during the summer months. It was hard work, but I could make lots of money working overtime and double time. It was often 16-20 hour days but a lot of money for a poor kid living on John's Island, SC. I saw many of my friends settle for that life; but I knew that was not my path. I knew that this life was not for me.

So I decided I was going to go to college and become an engineer. I was told it wasn't possible—that "it ain't no way you can be an engineer"—this is 1972 folks. But I didn't care what "they" thought. I knew what I wanted for my life. Said another way, I knew what I didn't want, so I went on to Tuskegee University, worked hard in my studies and earned my engineering degree and graduated with honors--cum laude.

But how many people have been told by others that they couldn't accomplish a particular goal. How many times did they hear, "that's not possible." How many were stopped by negative people. How many today, as grown adults, are allowing themselves to be kept down by the words of those naysayers? Stop surrounding yourself with the 99% who don't believe in your abilities. Focus on the 1%. Stop focusing on the 99% chance that you won't accomplish your goal. Focus on the 1% that you will. It's time to get up and start focusing on this 1% chance right now!

Stop! Take the time now to analyze your situation and figure out what is keeping you down. Provide responses to the following questions:

What are the things from the past or the thoughts and beliefs you hold that are keeping you from moving forward?

1.

2.

3.

4

5.

6.

7.

8.

9.

10.

Are you going in the wrong direction? If so, what are the things that you are doing that are taking you in the wrong direction?

1.

2.

3.

4.

5.

6.

7.

8.

9.

10.

If you are going in the wrong direction, what are the things that you need to do today, to make a U-turn and head in the right direction?

1.

2.

3.

4.

5.

6.

7.

8.

9.

10.

CHAPTER 8

What's stopping you from achieving your goal?

What is stopping you from achieving your goal? Is it your friends? Is it peer pressure? Is it your family? Is it you? Can you accurately identify the roadblocks to achieving your goal? I ask this question because sometimes what we think is a roadblock is really not the actual roadblock. The actual roadblock is entirely something different. You must take the time to study the whole problem, not just the parts where you think the issue is located.

Start with the whole problem and work towards identifying the root cause. Identify the things under your control that are stopping you from achieving your goals. If you want to start a physical fitness program, what's stopping you? Don't you know that you actually have the power to get up early and exercise—it may only require that you set your alarm? You also have the power to go to the gym or visit the local area track—you may be pleasantly surprised at how many people are on the local track in the early morning hours—let these new found fitness mates be your motivator. You have the power to take the steps necessary to achieve your goals. If we look closer, we will realize that it is usually "us" that are stopping our achievement.

It is our mentality that is stopping us from achieving our goal. I've said this before, you need to know your enemy, and you need to know yourself. A lot of times the enemy lies within—the enemy is you. Sometimes we are our own worst enemy. If you are your worst enemy, if you are the roadblock to achieving your goal, then you know exactly what I am going to say, "Stop, Analyze your situation and fix it, right now!"

Mental barriers

Lack of Desire - Some of us say we want to accomplish this, we want to accomplish that, we want to be this type of career person, but lack a true desire. Desire is the first step to accomplishing your goal. Without desire, we have no motivation to move forward when the going gets tough. What is desire? I would define desire at its root as love. Desire is a love for something or someone that is deeply rooted and immovable. Desire is the root of all great accomplishments. When I was in flight school and I failed the first exam twice, I could have easily given up; but I didn't because of desire, not only my own desire but the desire of my family to see me succeed, the desire of my wife to make sure I succeeded, the desire of my wife to make sure I stayed focused on the goal and her desire to help me study and study correctly. It is safe to say that this desire helped me keep going. You need to develop your desire and once you have it, you gotta do whatever you need to do to keep this desire burning and burning bright, not dim. Develop this desire in children early and monitor continuously for deviations.

Lack of Faith - Do you believe that you can accomplish what you're doing? As I mentioned earlier, faith is absolutely essential to you achieving your goal. Why would anyone move towards a goal that they didn't believe they could accomplish? Well, the answer is they would not. You need to ask yourself if you lack the faith in your abilities to accomplish the goals that you desire. If you do lack faith, take the time to find out why, and then change your mindset.

Without faith, I would not have been able to earn my bachelors degree in mechanical engineering. Without faith, I would not have graduated from undergraduate pilot training. I would not have been able to fly fast jets, large jets, in all kinds of weather, navigating by instruments ONLY because you can't see outside the cockpit (in other words, you can't see the ground!). It's ONLY through faith in these instruments, faith in a higher power, faith in God and faith in my abilities that I could fly under these conditions.

We were taught to "BELIEVE OUR INSTRUMENTS"—this takes a lot of faith especially when your body, your mind, your sense of balance, your equilibrium, wants to tell you something different like when your body says you are flying upside down, but the instruments say you are right side up—which do you believe? Putting your faith in the wrong thing, at the wrong time, with not much margin for error, could be catastrophic, could be deadly.

You must have faith and this faith comes from training--continuous training. This faith comes from believing...believing in yourself, believing in others, believing in your instruments. This faith comes from doing your homework, from doing your study, from networking with folks that do what you do, and I almost missed a BIGGIE, this faith comes from PRACTICE, sometimes years of PRACTICE, PRACTICE, PRACTICE; the type of practice that insures that your faith will not waiver, will never waiver when challenged by forces or events that could destroy you. Practice makes your faith strong. Continuous practice keeps your faith strong. Practice will bring you success. Without faith, I would not have written this book. Without faith, I would not have even started writing this book after being stuck in traffic for four months because I was going in the wrong direction trying to accomplish my goal to become a public speaker. Without faith, I would not have recognized that I could make a U-turn and get moving in the right direction. Without faith, you will not be able to get out of the traffic jam of your life.

Lack of Knowledge - Many of us set out to accomplish a goal completely ignorant of what we need to do to get there. Folks, everything in this book is related. If you go back to the chapters on establishing your goal, plans to achieve your goal, and doing all the right things to make sure you accomplish your goal, you will see that knowledge is such a vital part of making your goal a reality. Knowledge will allow you to realize whether or not you have the qualifications (physical, mental, financial, etc) to get up and make it happen. Knowledge will direct your actions. Lack of knowledge will get you blindsided by events, events that if you were aware of from the beginning of your journey, would not catch you off guard and would not let you be blindsided.

Let me introduce you to this statement, “Until there is awareness, there can be no consensus for change.” Let me say this again: “Until there is awareness, there can be no consensus for change”--except maybe by accident which in my opinion is no way to live your life or the life you want for your family.

If you don’t know that something is not good for you, if you don’t know that the direction you are taking will not get you to your destination, you will continue along that direction to no avail. In other words, you won’t do anything to fix it and you won’t get there. You must first know that you are going in the wrong direction before you can fix anything—awareness is the key!

If you don’t take the time to make yourself aware, if you don't take the time to study what it is that you want to accomplish, you will never know what it takes to get there. If we don't educate ourselves with the knowledge of how others accomplished what we are trying to do, we will most likely be caught “off guard” when there is really no reason for it. There is absolutely no reason to re-invent the wheel, to go through all the steps if some of the steps have already been done for you. You need to “Work smarter, not harder.” But the only way to do this is to become more aware, aware of as many things as possible related to what you are trying to do. Because we lack the knowledge necessary to make informed decisions, we continue “grabbing at straws” and going in the wrong direction.

Lack of Motivation - Maybe you just don't feel like doing what it takes to get what you want. Maybe you are tired or just feeling lazy. If this is you, you need to “get real” today, right now. A lot of us say we want to do something, become this significant person or become financially successful, but we aren’t doing any of the things necessary to make these goals a reality. Some of us are just too busy—too busy having fun, too busy watching TV or heaven forbid, too busy gossiping on the phone or sleeping our life away. We are just too busy distracted with other stuff that we never find the time or motivation to do the hard work to move forward. We need to get motivated in order to accomplish our goals and we need to do this right now.

Physical Barriers

Lack of Money - Do you lack the money necessary to accomplish your goals? Maybe you're experiencing extreme financial hardship. Do you feel like there's no way out of your financial hole? Well there is a way; it's just that you don't realize it yet.

You're not the first person to experience financial difficulty and I guarantee you that you will not be the last. Get educated on finances and budgeting issues today. Have you exhausted all the financial avenues available to you? What about attending free lectures and seminars in your local area, especially those put on by your local chamber of commerce and other civic organizations? Additionally, how do you personally define your local area?

Is it everything within 10 miles or can you expand your area to the next town/city? Can you expand your radius of action point to say anything within 40 miles from your home or better yet within a one-hour drive from your home? If you can do this, you will be exposing yourself to a much larger pool of financial resources and other networking opportunities that may be able to provide you with excellent alternatives or options to finance your career or business venture. If your circle of friends, business associates, classmates, people who want to achieve or make their life better by doing something about it is very, very, small, you can expect that your financial opportunities and options will also be very, very small or nonexistent. If you do anything at all, expand your circle—you will be pleasantly surprised.

And folks, if you are not using the internet to expand your circle, you are missing out on a truly valuable source of information, information from people all over the world. If you don't have a computer or access to the internet, please visit your local library, other establishments or maybe even get your job to allow you to have access to the internet, especially if it gives them a better employee. Start talking to folks who are financially successful and find a way to better your situation.

I am reminded here of a term I use very often when talking with audiences—the term is R^2A^2 taken from the book "The Science of Success" by Napoleon Hill--I paraphrase here for my purposes: RECOGNIZE opportunities when they reveal themselves to you—always be on the look out and always be prepared for these opportunities. Then seriously RELATE yourself to this opportunity—ask yourself these relationship questions: "Is this for me? Can I do this? Does this fit what I want to do? And next, I want you to ASSIMILATE someone or others in your area that are doing exactly what you are doing and are doing it very well. You can probably get them to mentor you and provide you insights as to how they achieved their goal. The last thing I want you to do is to ACT because if you don't ACT, the RECOGNIZE, RELATE and ASSIMILATE don't mean a thing—all you succeeded in doing is blowing smoke and doing nothing. Ya'll know the saying: Talk is Cheap!"

Illness and Bad Health – Now, this is an interesting subject. What is bad health? Does bad health also include mental issues? Can an illness be mental? Is yours a physical health issue or a mental issue? Are your health problems (physical or mental) stopping you from moving forward? Are you overweight, out of shape, suffering from ill health caused by a bad diet? Have you researched the appropriate medical care, if the problem is really a medical issue? If your problem is getting your body back in shape, have you researched fitness coaches or personal trainers? If your problem is eating the wrong food at the wrong time, what about consulting with a dietician? Or, after all the questions above, is your health issue the result of a bigger issue like your MOTIVATION or lack there of?

Then, you need to ask yourself, what's driving your lack of motivation? Is your health a symptom of a much bigger problem? Whatever this bigger issue is, you need to really sit down and try to identify it immediately because until you determine what this bigger issue is, these health issues will continue to be a roadblock to achieving your goal or accomplishing whatever task set before you.

Similarly folks, if your problem is a physical issue beyond your control that leaves you physically challenged, I definitely suggest seeking medical attention to help you to first cope with the challenge and accept it. I am absolutely amazed at folks who accept their physical challenges and go on to accomplish amazing things in their lives.

Folks, there is always someone worst off than you are and I know that this is much easier said than done, BUT the fact remains that some of these folks are making it happen for themselves. I personally use them as a motivational jumpstart when I am feeling sorry for myself.

This can also be extended to people with less credentials or qualifications than you have, BUT none the less are very successful at doing what they want to do with their life. Study these folks and ask yourself, why are they successful? Maybe it's because they have faith; maybe it's because they have desire; they have drive; they have motivation; and they believe in themselves.

Ladies and gentlemen, it is time to take control and realize that life can and must go on, so if you have the good fortune to continue to live, remember that time waits on no one. What better time than right now? Beethoven was deaf before he ever composed his first concerto. He did not allow physical disability to stop him from accomplishing his goals. If he did not, so can you!

Stop! Take time out and make a list of the things that are stopping you from accomplishing your goals.

1.

2.

3.

4.

5.

6.

7.

8.

9.

10.

Ask yourself, what is it that you can do today to overcome the mental and physical barriers standing between you and your goals?

1.

2.

3.

4.

5.

6.

7.

8.

9.

10.

CHAPTER 9

Don't Give Up!

Don't give up! Don't give up in your personal life and don't give up in your business life. Any goal you have that you want to accomplish is going to have some obstacles. Sometimes you're going to be "stuck in traffic" feeling like you're going nowhere fast. But you can't give up. Sometimes you're going to be going in the wrong direction and end up farther from your goal than when you first set out on your journey. But you can't give up. Sometimes it will look like everybody is against you; no one believes in you; and that the winds of good fortune are not blowing your way. But even then, you can't give up.

Henry Ford, one of America's greatest inventors, didn't give up. He spent most of his money, time and energy perfecting the "Model T". He went home at night with the "Model T" on his mind. He dismantled the Ford over and over and over again in his quest for perfecting the automobile. The people around him were astonished and amazed at his desire to be the best and some even thought he was too ambitious—maybe a little crazy. But look today, Ford is still around. Because Henry Ford did not give up in his pursuit to be the best that he could be, the Ford car is still one of the best selling automobiles in the world.

No matter what, you need to persist; you need to continue to press on; don't give up. Don't let minor or major setbacks stop you. Don't allow failures to discourage you. Most millionaires declared bankruptcy before achieving success and many of them did this more than a few times. Shut your ears to those negative people who tell you that you can't achieve your goal. They will "kick you" when you're down and "love you" when you are up.

Like you, many have faced what seemed like obstacles so big that they could not overcome them. I remember when I first arrived at Tuskegee University to pursue my engineering degree. I was confident, proud and I knew that I could do well. I knew that I was at my best, having graduated in the top 5% of my senior class from John's Island, SC. My goodness, I was voted “Best All Around” by my senior class mates—they believed I had all the “right stuff” to be successful. I was confident that I could accomplish anything.

As it turned out, however, I wasn't as prepared as I thought. I was really a little “old country boy” from the South and educated in the South. I hate to knock the South, (remember this is 1972) but a lot of the students in my Tuskegee University engineering class were from the northern states and most of them had already taken college level math which included calculus. Well, little old “country boy” me did not have any of these classes in my high school and if we did, I sure didn’t take advantage of any of these advanced classes.

I was behind and not just behind white students BUT behind other black students, black students from the north and black students from the south who were made aware early in their education process to take the right college preparatory courses. This was very frustrating for me. I hadn't studied what it took to become an engineer, so I hadn't taken the math classes necessary to move forward in my engineering studies immediately after arriving at college. So while I was busy playing catch up and taking prerequisite entry level math courses, my peers (I always considered myself in the top 5 percent) were on the fast track to getting their engineering degree in four years vice the 5-year schedule I was on--some taking calculus the first semester of our freshman year.

My ego was crushed. I felt crippled. The math classes I took in my first year didn't count towards my degree. The classes counted towards total college credits BUT it didn’t do anything for my mechanical engineering major.

I was discouraged. I could have given up. I could have changed majors, which was very tempting considering several of my classmates did just that. I could have said "this isn't fair, I give up." But I didn't. And because I didn't give up, I caught up with my peers, worked hard, stayed focus on my goal and received my mechanical engineering degree, graduating cum laude in the top 5% of my class.

When life hits you with obstacles and when you suffer from the consequences of not being prepared, you can't just stay down and cry, you got to get up and stay focused on your goal. Stay focused on the reason you are where you are and do the necessary things to finish what you started. I did and so can you!

Answer the following question as truthfully as you can.

What are some of the things you need to do to stay on track towards your goal?

1.

2.

3.

4.

5.

6.

7.

8.

9.

10.

Do you feel like giving up?

Before you throw your hands up and throw the towel in, ask yourself the following questions...

Have you done your homework? Did you study your goal thoroughly? If you haven't done your homework on your goal then you haven't given yourself a fighting chance and you are cheating yourself if you give up now. Look at your goals and ask yourself if you have thoroughly investigated what you say you want to do.

Have you followed your plan? Did you do everything in your power to accomplish your goal? Be honest. If your goal is to lose weight, did you exercise everyday and eat healthy food? No guess work. If you followed the instructions from earlier you know that you need to keep track of what it is that you're doing on a daily basis to accomplish your goals. Keeping a written record of your activities keeps you honest. If you haven't done everything in your power to accomplish your goal, then YOU DON'T HAVE THE RIGHT TO GIVE UP.

Have you given yourself enough time to accomplish your goal? How long did it take others to accomplish the thing that you are trying to achieve? Learn patience and be realistic in what you can accomplish in any given amount of time.

Making an informed decision on giving up?

The only valid reason for giving up is that you lack desire. Maybe you don't really want what it is that you say you want to accomplish. Go back and think about what your motivation is for pursuing your goal. Are you motivated by love? Or, are you motivated by fear, money, fame, power? Only desire or love can get you through the hard times of this life journey.

If you don't have love for what you are doing, you're going to give up. If you are pursuing a goal only because you think you can make a lot of money, you're going to give up. Get real about your motivation and if you realize that you do "have love" for the thing that you are trying to accomplish, then you should not give up.

You "should not" give up until you've exhausted all avenues and even then you need to give it a second and thorough thought.

When life's darkest moments descend upon you, don't give up.

When you think life is over, don't give up.

Stop! Take the time to analyze your situation and answer the following questions:

If you feel like giving up, what are your reasons for feeling this way?

1.

2.

3.

4.

5.

6.

7.

8.

9.

10.

What are the things that you haven't done that you should have done in the pursuit of your goal?

1.

2.

3.

4.

5.

6.

7.

8.

9.

10.

For the things that you haven't done that you should have done in the pursuit of your goals, take the time now to figure out a plan to do those things before you consider giving up. Tell yourself why you haven't done what it takes to accomplish your goals and create a simple and measurable way to implement those actions into your plan.

> *In a world where most people just go with the flow, never challenging the tide, it can be difficult to walk to the beat of your own drummer. But for those who dare to move confidently in the direction of their dreams there is a treasure awaiting you, not of gold or silver; but of happiness and a life fully lived. "Author Unknown"*

Don't Give Up Folks!

CONCLUSION

If you find that your life resembles being "Stuck in Traffic," I hope that by reading this book, you find a way to get yourself "Unstuck" and most of all, a means to avoid being stuck in the future. I hope that your life has been touched in some way; that you can identify with some of the chapter comments and that I have inspired you to start "right now" to make a positive difference in your life.

Read and discuss "Are You Stuck in Traffic?" with your significant other, your family and your friends.

Additionally, in Appendix A, a 1-page stand-alone handout, modified from my motivational TV series presentations, is provided for each chapter discussed in this book.

Appendix B provides additional information about The Saunders Executive Resources Group, LLC, sample seminar sessions, and a couple of homework assignments for those of you who want or need extra credit.

It's been my pleasure!

William R. Saunders
Colonel, USAF Retired

APPENDIX A: CHAPTER HANDOUTS

20 February 2006

Motivational Series: Are You Stuck in Traffic?—An Interesting Parallel to Life? An Interactive Approach

Description: Series of questions designed to provoke thought; to provoke action; to get you prepared for contingencies. Designed as a 5-minute teaser discussion--interactive; motivational and provocative.

- Have you ever been "Stuck in Traffic" and going no where?
- What about with your life? Your Goals? Your Plans? Your education? Your Dreams?
- What does "Stuck in Traffic" mean to you?
  - -- Same old Job/Relationship/Routine/Situation/etc
- Why are you stuck in traffic? Do you get stuck often? Are your friends stuck?
- Have you been "Stuck in Traffic" long? Do you care?
- Did you plan for it? Did you anticipate the traffic?
- What happens when you get stuck?
- Do you have a course of action? Do you have a plan?
- Have you done a cost-benefit analysis?
- Do you get frustrated? Are you frustrated now? Are you stuck now?
- Did you bring something with you to ease the frustration? Do you know where it is?
- What is available to ease your frustration?

THINGS YOU CAN DO:

- Pull out pen & paper and take an inventory of your life right now
- Determine what has you "Stuck in Traffic?"
- What can you change to prevent being stuck?
- What are some of the things you can do to avoid getting stuck?
- What are some of the things you can do when you find yourself stuck?
- Improve your position?
  - -- Know your priorities; do your homework, be early, study
  - -- School/vacation/relax/read/trade/etc
  - -- Let others help (spouse/kids/friends/family/professional/etc)
- Brainstorm all available options for before, during & after being stuck in life's traffic

Ladies and Gentlemen: Stop for a moment and analyze your situation. If you take the time to analyze your life, you may find that you can minimize being stuck in the traffic of life. This 1-page handout by Colonel Bill Saunders is provided for your use as a handy, stand-alone, quick reference guide to make you think; to provoke thought. There are no right or wrong answers and no judgment. Find ways to "Unstuck" yourself today—life is too precious to be "Stuck in Traffic!"

Objectives:

(1) Readers learn how to start the process of getting their life in order
(2) Readers learn how to anticipate/prepare for things that cause them to be stuck in traffic

Website: http://thesaundersexecutiveresourcesgroup.com/index.html; Email: bill.saunders@cox.net

Serviced Disabled Veteran-Owned Business
Currently Showcased: Forbes, Business Week and The AtlantaBizJournals On-Line Magazines

16 January 2006

Motivational Series: Are You the Best At What You Do? If Not, Why Not & What Are You Going to Do About it?—An Interactive Approach

Description: Series of comments & questions designed to provoke thought; to provoke action; to get you prepared for contingencies. Designed as a 5-minute teaser discussion--interactive; motivational and provocative.

- If you are the best, what are you doing to stay the best?
- Define the word best. Are you #1, #2, #3? Do you care?
- If you are not the best, what are you doing to make yourself the best?
- Do you need to go back to school? Do you need to go to training schools?
- Do you know where you are right now? Do you know where you are at?
- What are you doing about it? Who can you turn too? Who can help make a difference?
- Are you the best worker? Are you the best employee?
- What do you need to do to improve your position? To get you on the right track?
- Are you prepared to make yourself the best? Are you re-educating yourself?
- Are you talking to your friends? Are your friends helping you?
- Are you going back to school? Are you doing your Homework? Your study?
- What is your motivation for being the best? Do you really want to be the best?
- Where do you want to be in the scheme of things?
- Are you not motivated? Are you doing this for yourself? For someone else?

THINGS YOU CAN DO:
- You need to get yourself mentally prepared to make yourself the best--Whatever that is.
- Know yourself and your capabilities; know your strength; know your weaknesses
- Know thy enemies; know thyself; in most cases, you are your worst enemy
- Know the people most close to you are the ones who stop you from achieving your best
- Determine who is on your side and who is not
- Take the time to make yourself the best at whatever you want to be
- Take advantage of what's available to allow you to achieve your best
- It's time to stop all the excuses, all the reasons why you can't do something
- Know the things that are within your control (like study, attitude, etc)

Ladies and Gentlemen: Stop for a moment and analyze your situation--find ways to make yourself the best today! This 1-page handout by Colonel Bill Saunders is provided for your use as a handy, stand-alone, quick reference guide to make you think; to provoke thought. There are no right or wrong answers and no judgment--just be the best at what you do. It's been my pleasure.

Objectives:

(1) Readers learn how to start the process of making themselves the best at what they do
(2) Readers learn how to anticipate and prepare for things that impact their lives

Website: http://thesaundersexecutiveresourcesgroup.com/index.html; Email: bill.saunders@cox.net

Serviced Disabled Veteran-Owned Business
Currently Showcased: Forbes, Business Week and The AtlantaBizJournals On-Line Magazines

23 January 2006

Motivational Series: What is Your Goal, Your Starting Point? Connect the Two; Believe It & You Can Achieve It—An Interactive Approach

Description: Series of comments & questions designed to provoke thought; to provoke action; to get you prepared for contingencies. Designed as a 5-minute teaser discussion--interactive; motivational and provocative.

- What is your goal? Is it your goal? Is it someone else's goal?
- Where is your starting point? Where are you right now?
- Is your goal realistic? Achievable? Is it doable? Does it make sense to you?
- Are you qualified? Is this something you really want to do?
- What are the roadblocks to achieving your goal? Is it money? Is it time? Is it others?
- Can you move these roadblocks? Do you need help moving these roadblocks?
- Do you believe you can achieve this goal? Do you understand the goal?
- Are you prepared to do what it takes to achieve your goal?
- What are the things you need to do to make your self qualified?
- Are you motivated? Are you tired? What is it?
- Are you procrastinating? Are you sitting on yesterday's wins?
- Do you have Clarity of Purpose with your life?

THINGS YOU CAN DO:

- Find a quiet spot and brainstorm what your goal is—know your goal today
- Share your goal with your significant other/trusted friend & solicit support
- Write down the things you need to do in chronological order to make the goal a reality
- Make sure you know where your starting point is—then connect to your end point (goal)
- Seriously ask yourself if you truly believe that you can achieve this goal
- It's time to put your life in order; to take inventory of your life
- Stay focused on your goal--get rid of the things that hinder you from achieving the goal
  -- You know what I am talking about—those friends, those extracurricular activities

Ladies and Gentlemen: It's Time to have a goal that is realistic and achievable. Stop for a moment and analyze your goal; Is it still realistic given today's technology and relationships? This 1-page handout by Colonel Bill Saunders is provided for your use as a handy, stand-alone, quick reference guide to make you think; to provoke thought. There are no right or wrong answers and no judgment. Define your goal today.

Objectives:

(1) Readers learn how to start the process of defining their goal
(2) Readers learn how to anticipate and prepare for things that impact their lives

Website: http://thesaundersexecutiveresourcesgroup.com/index.html; Email: bill.saunders@cox.net

Serviced Disabled Veteran-Owned Business

Currently Showcased: Forbes, Business Week and The AtlantaBizJournals On-Line Magazines

30 January 2006

Motivational Series: What is Your Plan to Achieve Your Goal? Is it realistic? Is it Your Plan?—An Interactive Approach

Description: Series of questions designed to provoke thought; to provoke action; to get you prepared for contingencies. Designed as a 5-minute teaser discussion--interactive; motivational and provocative.

- Do you have a plan? Where is it? When is the last time you looked at your plan?
- Is it your plan? Is it someone else's plan? Is the plan normal for you?
- Can you achieve the actions designed by the plan?
- What are the priorities for you? Can you prioritize the task?
- If you don't have a plan, what are you doing to put your plan to action?
- Do you have a back-up plan?
- What is your course of action?
- What are the steps? How many steps?
- Is it a normal plan for you? Is your plan in line with your goals?
- Is your plan prioritized? How many things are on your plate?
- What things can come off your plate?
- What are the competing tasks? Which task comes first? How many tasks are there?
- What is your motivation to achieve your plan?

THINGS YOU CAN DO:
- Relate your plan to others doing what you want to do BUT DOING IT VERY WELL
- Do your study; do your homework?
- Make sure your plan makes sense for you, especially as it relates to your goal
- Don't sugar coat what you want to do; don't pacify yourself
- Believe in the plan; Believe in yourself; Act now to put a plan in place
- Modify the plan as required
- It's Time to put balance in your life; to know & take care of your priorities

Ladies and Gentlemen: It's time to put a plan of action in place! This 1-page handout by Colonel Bill Saunders is provided for your use as a handy, stand-alone, quick reference guide to make you think; to provoke thought. There are no right or wrong answers and no judgment. Put together a plan that allows you to achieve your goal.

Objectives:

(1) Readers learn how to start the process of putting a plan of action in place
(2) Readers understand the importance of having a plan to achieve their goal

Website: http://thesaundersexecutiveresourcesgroup.com/index.html; Email: bill.saunders@cox.net

Serviced Disabled Veteran-Owned Business
Currently Showcased: Forbes, Business Week and The AtlantaBizJournals On-Line Magazines

6 February 2006

Motivational Series: Are You Prepared To Tell Me Who You Are in 30 Seconds? An Interactive Approach

Description: Series of questions designed to provoke thought; to provoke action; to get you prepared for contingencies. Designed as a 5-minute teaser discussion--interactive; motivational and provocative.

- Do you know who you are? Can you tell me who are you? Can you do it in 30 Seconds?
- What value do you bring to the table?
- Why should I hire you over someone else?
- What makes you so different?
- What differentiates you from the next candidate?
- Can you tell me what you want me to know about you in 30 seconds?
- Can you articulate/communicate what you have provided on paper? Not on paper?
    - -- 100 candidates, 3 jobs, you made top 10% BUT all paperwork looks the same
    - -- CEO, Interviewer, Client, don't have time to read but will make a decision
    - -- If called, do you already know what you want to say?
- Can you communicate succinctly, specifically, quantifiable who you are?
- Do you understand where I am going here?
- Can you market yourself in 30 seconds? With Specificity? With Accuracy?
- Why should a potential client purchase your product, your service, or hire you?
- Tell Me right now—you have 30 seconds, so don't waste it: Go Ahead, I am listening
- Did this question or questions catch you of guard? If it did, Why? What does this mean?

THINGS YOU CAN DO:

- Don't allow yourself to be caught of guard
- Always anticipate this question
- Practice, Practice, Practice until you get it just right; make it 2nd nature
- Practice in front of the mirror, your kids, your friends, your spouse
- Make sure you are prepared
- Do your homework; do your study
- Analyze your audience: potential client, customers, employer, etc
- Get yourself ready

Ladies and Gentlemen, make sure you can tell folks who you are without mistakes. This 1-page handout by Colonel Bill Saunders is provided for your use as a handy, stand-alone, quick reference guide to make you think; to provoke thought. There are no right or wrong answers and no judgment. Now, can you tell me who you are in 30 seconds?

Objectives:

(1) Readers learn self-confidence and how to prioritize
(2) Readers learn significance of not being caught off guard; of being prepared

Website: http://thesaundersexecutiveresourcesgroup.com/index.html; Email: bill.saunders@cox.net

Serviced Disabled Veteran-Owned Business
Currently Showcased: Forbes, Business Week and The AtlantaBizJournals On-Line Magazines

13 February 2006

Motivational Series: So You Are Too Busy—Tell Me Why You Are So Busy? An Interactive Approach

Description: Series of questions designed to provoke thought; to provoke action; to get you prepared for contingencies. Designed as a 5-minute teaser discussion--interactive; motivational and provocative.

- Why are you so busy? What makes you so busy? Tell me why?
- Who are you that your life is so busy you can't respond to something w/i 24-48 hours?
- Who is controlling your time? Is it the boss? Is it You?
- Is it the kids? What is it? What has got you so busy? Are you watching too much TV?
- Are you spending too much time doing non-productive things during the day?
- Have you dissected your day? What do you do all day? What are you doing right now?
- What are your priorities? What are your needs? What are your wants?
- Is your life in BALANCE? How do you put it all in balance?
- What are the things that can be eliminated? How much time do you gain?
- What excess baggage are you carrying? How long have you been carrying this excess?
- Are you volunteering too much of your services? How many outside organizations?
- Do you know excess baggage, as in excess inventory, costs you MONEY and TIME?
- Are you too busy to go back to school? To get a certificate, training?
- Are you too busy to put your life in order? In Balance? Too busy to play with the kids?
- Are you too busy to take your spouse/significant other to lunch or dinner?

THINGS YOU CAN DO:

- Take an inventory of your life right now
- Pull out pen and paper and write down everything you do each day
- BRAINSTORM this list: don't try to analyze this lists right now, get it down on paper
- Don't short change yourself either; include everything you do
- Prioritize this list into MUST DO (Needs) and WOULD LIKE TO DO (Wants)
- Now take a look at what can be Eliminated or Moved to another day

Ladies and Gentlemen: Stop for a moment and analyze your situation; If you take the time to analyze your life, you may find that you can make the time to take care of you, your family, etc. Life is too short to be so busy everyday of the week. Take something of your plate today. Learn how to "SAY NO" when and where you can! This 1-page handout by Colonel Bill Saunders is provided for your use as a handy, stand-alone, quick reference guide to make you think; to provoke thought. There are no right or wrong answers and no judgment. Stop being so busy!

Objectives:

(1) Readers learn the importance of prioritizing activities that impact their lives
(2) Readers learn the significance of Time Management

Website: http://thesaundersexecutiveresourcesgroup.com/index.html; Email: bill.saunders@cox.net

Serviced Disabled Veteran-Owned Business

Currently Showcased: Forbes, Business Week and The AtlantaBizJournals On-Line Magazines

6 March 2006

Motivational Series: It's Time To Get Up—Not Later But Right Now!—An Interactive Approach

Description: Series of questions designed to provoke thought; to provoke action; to get you prepared for contingencies. Designed as a 5-minute teaser discussion--interactive; motivational and provocative.

- Why are you still sitting down when you have things to do?
- Are you not motivated? Are you tired? What is it?
- It's Time to get up; No more procrastination; No more sitting on yesterday's wins
- It's Time to make that Goal a reality; it's time to Act; it's time to Execute
- It's Time to have Clarity of Purpose with your life; read the book "A Purpose-Driven Life"
- It's Time to make yourself the best at what you do
- It's Time to Rise Up above being "Just OK." Just a regular guy/gal
- It's Time to make your self stand out; In the Work place, In Class; Be the Best
- It's Time to go back to school if you need too
- It's Time to stop going in the wrong direction; especially when you know it
- If you are going in the wrong direction with your life; your family; your career; your job; your children; your health, your friends, YOU NEED TO STOP, STOP RIGHT NOW!
- The Results: The Goal that you want will not be achieved if you continue along this path
- You need to change direction and you need to do it today, RIGHT NOW!
- It's Time to put your life in order; it's time to take inventory of your life
- It's time to get rid of those excess things that take you away from achieving your goal -- You know what I am talking about—those friends, things that bring you NO VALUE
- It's Time to Stop all the excuses, all the reasons why you can't do something
- It's Time to take care of those things that are within your control (like study, attitude, etc)
- It's Time to look at HOW TO make things happen & STOP looking at How NOT TO
- If there is a 1%, 5% chance of making it happen, put your energy in this 1%, 5%
- It's Time to stop wasting your time with the 95% nay sayers; work with the 5%
- It's Time to put balance in your life; it's time to know & take care of your priorities

Ladies and Gentlemen: It's Time to get up! Stop for a moment and analyze your habits; are you sitting down on the job? your life? Well, if you are, STOP IT!; Don't short change your life or your family; make the changes; get up right now and live your life the way it should be lived. Put your life in balance. This 1-page handout by Colonel Bill Saunders is provided for your use as a handy, stand-alone, quick reference guide to make you think; to provoke thought. There are no right or wrong answers and no judgment. Get up and act right now!

Objectives:

(1) Readers learn how to start the process of getting the maximum benefits out of life
(2) Readers learn how to anticipate and prepare for things that impact their lives

Website: http://thesaundersexecutiveresourcesgroup.com/index.html; Email: bill.saunders@cox.net

Serviced Disabled Veteran-Owned Business

Currently Showcased: Forbes, Business Week and The AtlantaBizJournals On-Line Magazines

13 March 2006

Motivational Series: What's Stopping You from Achieving Your Goal?—Identifying the Things Within Your Control!—An Interactive Approach

<u>Description</u>: Series of questions designed to provoke thought; to provoke action; to get you prepared for contingencies. Designed as a 5-minute teaser discussion--interactive; motivational and provocative.

- Do you know what's stopping you from achieving your goals? Do you care?
- What are the roadblocks to achieving your goal?
- Is it your Friends? Is it Peer pressure? Is it your Family? Is it You? Is it money?
- What is your economic status? Do you care? Can you do something about it?
- How is the job market where you live? Can you get the right job? Why not?
- Is education holding you back? Do you need to go back to school?
- Have you truly taken the time to evaluate the roadblocks to achieving your goal?
- Is your attitude the problem? What about your friend's attitude? Your Family?
- Are you motivated? Are you tired? What is it? Do you get enough rest?
- Is it your health? Are you physically/mentally able to achieve the goal?
- Are you procrastinating on your own or is someone else causing the procrastination?
- Have you analyzed your life for the moment, the day, for the week, the rest of your life?
- Why don't you or can't you control the things within your control?

THINGS YOU CAN DO?

- Brainstorm/Identify the things stopping you from achieving, no matter how small
- TAKE CHARGE--identify those things within your control and take care of them
- Use the things within your control to your advantage, not to your disadvantage.
- Solicit feedback from a friend, a co-worker, a teacher, a supervisor
- Seek wise counsel, if required
- Take inventory of your life & get rid of those excess things that bring you no value
- It's Time to Stop all the excuses, all the reasons why you can't do something
- Look at how to make things happen & STOP looking at How NOT to make it happen

Ladies and Gentlemen: Take charge of your life! Do it today, Right now. Don't short change your life or your family; Be responsible for the things within your control--make the changes right now that will put you on the right track to achieving your goal. This 1-page handout by Colonel Bill Saunders is provided for your use as a handy, stand-alone, quick reference guide to make you think; to provoke thought. There are no right or wrong answers and no judgment. Identify and eliminate the roadblocks in you life today.

Objectives:

(1) Readers learn how to start the process of taking charge of their destiny
(2) Readers learn how to identify roadblocks to achieving their goal

Website: http://thesaundersexecutiveresourcesgroup.com/index.html; Email: bill.saunders@cox.net

Serviced Disabled Veteran-Owned Business

Currently Showcased: Forbes, Business Week and The AtlantaBizJournals On-Line Magazines

27March 2006

Motivational Series: Don't Give Up!—An Interactive Approach

<u>Description</u>: Series of questions designed to provoke thought; to provoke action; to get you prepared for contingencies. Designed as a 5-minute teaser discussion--interactive; motivational and provocative.

- What exactly is the definition of "Giving Up?
    - -- Does it mean to quit, to stop, to fall down, to give in (in Life and in Business)?
- Do you give up when you still have the ability to make it?
- Do you give up when you still have time to get it right, to get on track?
- When should you give up? At what point should you give up?
    - -- Is it after exhausting all the facts?
    - -- Is it after doing everything within your power, within your control?
        - --- Do you know what's within your control?
    - -- Is it after doing all the right things? After analyzing your situation?
    - -- Is it after adding up all the plusses and minuses?
    - -- Is it after some serious sole searching, attitude check, Gut check?
    - -- Is it after realizing that doing all of the above still results in failure, etc?

THINGS YOU CAN DO:

- Pause, think, yield, take a time out, hack the clock, wait a minute
- Consider why you are quitting? Consider why are you giving up?
- Is it because you should not have started? Did you start with the right motivation?
- If you don't have to make the decision to quit today, don't make it
    - -- Make sure you know how much time is left (days, weeks, months, etc)
    - -- Make sure you know your limitations; Clint Eastwood said it well:
        - --- A man's gotta know his limitation! Do you know yours?
        - --- You gotta know when to fold em and when to hold em!
- Make sure you are prepared; what are the things you need to GET PREPARED?
- Do your study; do your homework; stay physically/mentally fit; stay healthy & rest
- Don't give up before exhausting all avenues available and I mean all avenues
- Everyday you get up brings you something; Make sure you get this new something!

Ladies and Gentlemen: Stop, Think and Analyze your situation thoroughly. If you can just wait a moment, life might just surprise you. This 1-page handout by Colonel Bill Saunders is provided for your use as a handy, stand-alone, quick reference guide to make you think; to provoke thought. There are no right or wrong answers and no judgment. Don't Give Up" until it's time!

Objectives:

(1) Readers learn to process all information before making decisions to quit
(2) Readers learn the importance of making a timely, wise decision

Website: http://thesaundersexecutiveresourcesgroup.com/index.html; Email: bill.saunders@cox.net

Serviced Disabled Veteran-Owned Business
Currently Showcased: Forbes, Business Week and The AtlantaBizJournals On-Line Magazines

APPENDIX B: ADDITIONAL INFORMATION

Join **Colonel Bill Saunders** for a **Powerful Motivational Seminar.**

Join **Colonel Bill Saunders** for a **Powerful Motivational Seminar.**

Join **Colonel Bill Saunders** for a **Powerful Motivational Seminar.**

For information regarding lectures, workshops, seminars, keynotes or ordering books, audio CDs or DVDS by the author, please visit my website, call, email or write:

William R. Saunders, Colonel, USAF Retired
P.O. Box 26095
Macon GA 31210
Email: bill.saunders@cox.net
478-320-9172

Website:
http://www.TheSaundersExecutiveResourcesGroup.com/index.html

<u>HOMEWORK</u>

<u>PROVIDE A LIST OF PEOPLE "**YOU KNOW**" BUT "**DON'T KNOW YOU**"</u>

1.

2.

3.

4.

5.

6.

7.

8.

9.

10.

HOMEWORK CONTINUED

NOW, PROVIDE A LIST OF PEOPLE "**WHO KNOW YOU**" OR YOU WANT "**TO KNOW YOU**" THAT CAN MAKE A DIFFERENCE IN YOUR LIFE (i.e. President, Mayor, CEO, GM, Senior Management, Secretary, Pastor, Commander, Colonel, Associate, Relatives, etc)

1.

2.

3.

4.

5.

6.

7.

8.

9.

10.

NOTE PAGE: THINGS TO DO

1.

2.

3.

4.

5.

6.

7.

8.

9.

10.

NOTE PAGE: THINGS TO CONSIDER

1.

2.

3.

4.

5.

6.

7.

8.

9.

10.